Kyle M.A. Fuhrer

Conquest: Budgeting and Becoming Debt-free on Low Income

I0465281

Table of Contents

Introduction

For many, financial freedom and a debt-free lifestyle may seem like an onerous if not impossible task. The sense of being utterly trapped by debt and personal financial responsibilities is only amplified when you are scraping out a merger income or are a low income earner. If you have ever done research into personal finances and debt repayment, you will quickly come to understand that most books are targeted at middle to higher income earners making the

advice all but irrelevant to lower income earners. It is my hope that this book will help people with low income find solutions to becoming debt-free and truly living their lives – a life of

financial freedom.

Through the process of reading this book you

will be introduced to several popular debt

repayment ideas and strategies and ultimately be

able to create personalized methods that will apply

to your particular financial situation. The methods

described in this book will work even if you are in the

situation where all your immediate bills are paid but

there is no money left over or worse yet, you do not

have enough money to even make your minimum

payments. Working from ground zero makes things

extremely difficult. I acknowledge that this task will

not be an easy one nor will your problems be solved

overnight. However, the aim of this book is to

provide you with fundamental tools and knowledge

to begin the process. In the pages that

follow, you will learn to create a financial game plan

and successfully execute it, to pay off your debt and

ultimately live a life free from fretting over how you

will pay off the next big crisis.

My Background

I'd like to share with you a little bit of information about my background. The point of this sharing is not to brag about my achievements or financial successes in life – to set myself up as some type of financial guru. On the contrary, it is simply to tell you that I know where you are coming from. I have firsthand knowledge from having lived in debt and having been a low income earner. As well, to inform you that I started the process of becoming debt-free even when I couldn't afford my minimum payments and despite this, I was still able to get ahead.

Everyone's situation is different with different pressures and responsibilities, but by being knowledgeable and calculated we are all able to achieve the same goal (NO MORE DEBT!). When I began my journey toward becoming debt-free it was 2010. I had recently been laid off at my job, I had two maxed out overdrafts, a maxed out credit card, two maxed out lines of credit, owed my parents somewhere in neighbourhood of ten thousand dollars, my car had broken down and my savings account had been scammed by an on-line hacker who withdrew all of my remaining money and savings. Point being, I was incredibly broke. I also had a huge student loan and a degree in a field that – due to a turbulent economy – no longer offered jobs opportunities. To make things worse, I suffered from a sense of entitlement that told me that I should be in a high level job that pays a good salary. After all, I had just spent the past five years in post-secondary education. This sense of entitlement ensured that I would stay unemployed for longer then I needed to be (because I would refuse opportunities if they weren't in my field). So, after 10 months of unemployment the bank threating repossession and the fear of bankruptcy looming over me, I took whatever job I could get. That meant working for minimum wage (at the time, less than $10 an hour). Now here is where things got tough and interesting. Working 40 hours a week earning less than $10 an hour meant that I couldn't make the minimum payments on my bills. I certainly couldn't maintain my previous lifestyle when faced with rent, vehicle repairs, food, utilities – you catch my drift. I calculated my debt to income ration and it was horrendous. It would take 116 percent of what I earned to cover the minimums on all of my expenses. Logic would dictate that either I get a second job or a better job in order to stay afloat. Guess what? I did neither yet was still able to pay off my debt.

From this point forward, I will explain exactly how I did it and how you can do it too! And if you are doing better than I was, good for you – this is going to be even easier for you. If your circumstances sound close to what I was dealing with then don't fret. Just keep reading and I will provide you with a number of simple yet powerful strategies that will deliver you from debt and allow you to start living – and thriving – again. Ready? Good. Let's get started.

Breaking Your Debt Addiction

The title of the chapter should be a dead giveaway as to what we will be sharing here. Creating more debt is an addiction and before you can make any progress on getting out of it, you need to stop being addicted to it. Addiction as defined by the Merriam dictionary is "an

unusually great interest in something or a need to do or have something." Think about that. Why is it that you are in debt in the first place? It is because of your interested

(myself included) in having things and doing stuff. Needs that are so strong that you have

created a dire situation in which you have amassed

debts in order to be able to attain said stuff or things, at the expense of your future, health and long-term goals. So the first thing to figure out is what is it that you need so badly and why do you need it. This could be anything such as a love to shop, eat out, buy the newest and best, upgrade things, impress people, substance abuse such as drinking, smoking or gambling, creating a perceived lifestyle. Anything and everything you can imagine could be part of this scenario.

Often financial books tell you that once you figure out what the spending habit/problem is, you need to stop it immediately. But the reality is that any addiction is best cured by slowly weaning yourself off it. However, if you can manage to stop cold turkey then more power to you. Go ahead and do it. Understand that under no circumstance am I saying do not change your behaviours. What I am trying to say is to start altering and questioning your behaviours and habits. There are people who have stopped smoking cold turkey but in reality that method rarely works for most people.

Figure out what it is that is eating up all of your money and driving you into debt and write it down on a piece of paper and carry it with you, then tell yourself how much you are going to reduce it by. Think of it as a workout in responsibility. Have you ever done a workout routine where you tell yourself you will do one push up a day and then add one more each day? Do the same with debt. Figure out the problem and make a goal to reduce it by X after every day, week and/or month –

whatever it is that you are comfortable with to start. And as you

become more comfortable with the reductions, try to accelerate the removal of the bad habit. For example, you eat out five times a week so the following week reduce that to 4 times, then the preceding week make it a maximum of three times and fairly soon, It is only once a month or once every two month and so on and so forth. A commonly accept notion is that it takes 21 days to create a habit so you want to get into the mindset of making self-improvement a habit. If you start off small it is easier to create and reinforced positive habits and then easier to achieve more difficult goals later on if you have already had previous successes.

But what about peer-pressure from family and friends? You have lots of friends who are always asking you out to do things that cost money. What you need to learn here is that it is OK to say no. It sounds insane but telling people you cannot afford the expense of going out or

doing that particular activity is far more widely accepted then you think. Also you can generally come up with a cheaper alternative. In truth, it is crazy expensive to go out all the time and it is a lot cheap to invite people over and do things at your place or at theirs.

You do not need to give up a fun lifestyle to save money. What you need to give up is an expensive lifestyle. You do not need to go out and blow cash in order to have a good time. Good friends will understand that and are still willing to hang out with you and have a great time without it costing a pile of cash. And if they don't, you need to question with whom you frequent and decide if they may be part of the problem.

The final point I want to touch on here is accepting responsibility. When it comes to debt it is easy to blame it on others or a certain situation or set of circumstances, (trust me I know, because I did it) but the truth of the matter is that you created the debt and thus created the problem. Plain and simple, if you cannot accept responsibility for the situation then you are not going to be able to fix the situation. For some, this may sound a lot harder than it is in reality. Honestly, all you need to do is figure out your debt load and say to yourself, "This is my fault and my problem. I created it now how do I fix it?" or "My debt is my responsibility. How do I pay it off?" Try saying it out load. It sounds weird but accepting responsibility feels good because it sets up a situation where you can acknowledge that there is a problem. It also puts the power for its resolution back into your hands. Choose not to be a victim but instead be a proactive hero and take charge of your life.

Figure it out and Write it down

It is time for the dreadful phrase: create a budget. I know what you are thinking, tracking all your receipts, recording everything you purchased and list it all out sounds like such a drag. Well, you are in luck because there are two different methods that we will be discussing in this chapter. The two methods that we will be discussing are what I like to call Write it down Light and Write it down Hard. Regardless of what you think about it, you need to create a budget of some sort because if you are not properly tracking your finances you will not be affectively in pay off your debts, nor will you no were your money is going.

Let's start off by looking at your traditional budget, aka, Write it down Hard. Begin by check through your most recent bank statement or statements in order to see o what you spend your money. If you are a cash only person, collect all of your receipts over the course of a month and then work out a spread sheet of everything you bought. Once you have determined where your money is being spent you will hopefully have a Eureka moment and likely say

something like, "Holy crap! I didn't know I was spending so much money on X, Y, and Z." Once you know where your money has been going, you can adjust your spending habits to reduce X, Y, and Z.

Write it down Light is a method where you do not have the will power and or time to track everything that you purchased for the month so instead you go straight into creating a budget. In this method you are going to figure out all of your minimum payments on everything and I mean everything. What does your housing cost, what are your minimum bill payments, what is your food cost (since you went with Write it Down Light you are going to have to guesstimate), your gas cost and so on. First, you need to figure out the minimums on all your expenses. Once you have this determined this, you should be left with a remaining amount of money. Keep in mind, this should be all your expenses prior to food and entertainment costs. Now, you need to factor in your food and entertainment budget, however, the budgeted amount must be less than the total remaining money in the budget (you need to have money left over after everything is factored in so as to have something to pay towards your bills, over and above your minimums) . The similarities between Write it Down Light and Write it Down Hard is that you are currently spending all of your monthly income but need to know where it is being spent and why. Once you know where your money is going you will have the ability to reduce your spending in a particular area (e.g. eating out too much or buying too many clothes) and reallocate that money towards your debt repayment.

Just to beat you over the head with this, you cannot skip this step, YOU HAVE TO HAVE A

WRITTEN DOWN BUDGET! The Write it Down Light version is the easiest way to do it, but

regardless or which method you choose, you must create a budget. Without one you will be unable to determine where your money is being spent and what your money is being spent on. Without this information you will not be able to improve your financial situation.

An appropriate question at this point would certainly be: With an income to debt ratio of 116 percent, how in the heck did I manage to pay anything off without earning more money? Well, part of the solution came from a piece of information imparted to me by my father. It solved a huge dilemma of mine and it will likely help solve a lot of problems for you, too. Plain and simple, under no circumstance do bank want you to go bankrupt or miss a payment. If you do, they don't make any money. As a result, most banks are willing to negotiate with you on minimums and payment schedules. For example, an average credit card rate starts at 19-21 percent. The bank only charges this rate because you have not asked for a better rate. Really. Even with a crap credit score, I was still able to get my interest rates down to 5-7 percent. I will discuss a few tactics for reducing your minimum interest rates later in this chapter. I will also provide a few ideas on what to do if the bank is unwilling to negotiate or reduce your interest rate. Two incredibly simple methods I have used are calling the banks 24-hour hotline and

asking for a lower interest rate and going to the help desk at your local bank branch and asking for a lower interest rate. Yup, that is pretty much all I did and it worked.

The first time I went into negotiate my minimums it was incredibly easy. However, this is not always the case. I called the bank and stated that 21 percent interest was insane and that there was no way I could ever cover the minimums and could they do better. The person on the phone said, "How does 11 percent sound?" Well, 11 percent sounded freaking amazing. Just think about how much of a different 10 percent makes. If you have a $5000 maxed-out credit card at 21 percent, you are paying roughly $87.50 a month on interest meaning your monthly minimums are around $100 a month, as opposed to at 11 percent where your minimum interest is roughly $45.33 or a minimum payment of about $50-55 a month. So at 21 percent you pay around $1,200 a year on your credit card of which $1050 is interest. In contrast, at 11 percent you will pay around $600-655 a year of which $543.96 is interest. That means that in interest alone you are saving roughly $504.06 a year. That is a lot of money, people! This is also assuming that you have only one credit card.

So what if you have several credit cards? It sounds crazy but asking your bank about a consolidated loan is likely your best option. Having two lines of credit (aka consolidated loans) I know that this is a good approach. Let me add a disclaimer and that being, if done correctly. If you just max out your cards again, you are likely going to end up with a second line of credit like I did and that is not a good thing. Make sure that if you do end up consolidating your debt that all other credit cards or financing cards are cancelled immediately after the consolidation loan comes into effect. A consolidated loan will almost always have a lower interest rate (unless your bank is particularly evil). You can move all of your credit card and overdraft debt to one loan instead of paying on multiple loans and pay a uniformed interest rate.

Now why wouldn't most people just do this and solve their problem? Well, the problem is that they do but they still have an addiction to debt, so guess what happens? Just like I did, they re-max out the paid-off credit cards and overdrafts and now also have a consolidated loan on top of all the other debt.

Now what if your bank is playing hard ball and will not drop your interest rate or consolidate your debt? Well, again it is easier than you think. We live in a world that is completely subjective. The secret is getting in touch with the right person at the finance office or bank and if no-one is willing to help you, shop around at other banks. Most banks will offer you a better rate in order to steal your business away from your current bank and if your

current bank is not willing to negotiate then good riddance – find a bank that will. So if the first person says no, ask to speak to someone different or call back the next day. Rinse and repeat until you get results. If you went to one bank that said no, chances are there are other branches you can visit that will help you out. Remember, when trying to reduce your interest rates, do not be demanding or aggressive as people are generally more willing to assist you if you are well spoken and have done your homework first. The only time that this starts to get exceptionally difficult is when you have already successfully negotiated your rate down several times. I found that getting your interest rate decreased the first time from 19-21 percent to 15-11 percent was fairly easy. But once you start getting your interest rate closer to the rate of prime the bank is generally less willing to help out. Prime refers to the rate the bank is paying to the government, thus, if you are paying a prime rate the bank is no longer making any money off you. However, this simply tactic I described kept working for me even when I had already reduced my interest rates down to 5 percent. 5 percent that was only prime + 2 percent that means that after the government has taken their 3 percent cut the bank only made 2 percent interest on me. Several times, by shopping around and continuously asking, I was also able to receive grace periods on interest. The grace periods were generally zero percent interest for 3 months. What this meant is the bank was giving me zero percent interest for 3 or more months at a time. As an example, on a $5000 credit card balance at 5 percent my interest payment is zero dollars and my monthly cost is only $4.77. Thus, 100 percent of that $4.77 went directly against the principal.

Once you have successful negotiated an interest drop, you need to wait a while before trying again. Do not try calling every week after a successful drop as the bank will likely make a note of this and start stonewalling you. If you get a 1 percent drop and two weeks later you are calling again, chances are you are not going to get anywhere. What I found best is if you wait 3 months and then try again. Once you get your interest rate low enough it will become harder and harder to get a lower rate but every once and a while you are likely to get a sweetheart "rate" deal which will again make a big difference toward paying off your debts.

At this point, I'd like to explain a couple banking traps you can fall into and how to avoid them. Banks have several deadly minimum fees that nickel and dime and chip away at your hard-earned money. One of the worst culprits is the dreaded overdraft scam. I like to refer to overdraft as a banking trick used to keep you broke forever. Years ago, I had two accounts with overdraft. One with $1500 of overdraft and a second with $500 and both accounts were maxed out. Just to have overdraft –

let alone use it — will typically cost you somewhere between $3 and $5 per month. This initial fee is just for the bank allowing you the privilege of having this service. Thus, if you have two overdrafts you are paying roughly $72 to $120 a year just for this service. In essence, you are paying the bank a fee in order to keep yourself broke. Great for the bank and not so great for you. However, the banks desire to gouge and screw does not end there. You are also going to be required to pay a minimum on your overdraft which is roughly 10 percent. The interest rate is not always 10 percent. In some cases, banks will charge as much as 24 percent interest on your overdrafts. Figure out what you are paying start trying to reduce those rates. On $2000 you will pay $16.66 in pure interest per month, not to mention the

minimum rate of repayment which would be another

$5 so you are already at $24.66 to $26.66 per month

minimum on your overdraft alone. And it does not

stop there. The bank also has an option known as

overdraft protection which ranges between $2 and

$4 per month. For every transaction you make while

in overdraft you will pay an additional of $1 to $5

fee.

Now, here is the trick with overdraft, if you

do not have it, do not get it. If you do have it, get rid

of it. The bank is merely tricking you into having

overdraft. It literally does nothing for you. It does

very little toward helping your credit score and is not

a good safety net for "just in case" expenses.

Overdraft is an all-around bad idea. A common

approach the bank uses to keep you in overdraft is to tell you that you need to pay off your overdraft all off at once. This, my friend, is total BS. In fact, you can reduce your overdraft at any time by any amount you desire. So, if you have a spare $5, reduce your overdraft by that much. Overdraft is an option you do not want. You will get eaten alive by the minimum charges that come along with it.

Overdraft protection on the other hand is something different. In fact, if you do not have overdraft protection, put this book down and call your bank right now and get overdraft protection. For me, I started out without overdraft protection and was paying roughly $30 a month in fees on-top of my monthly chargers which were in the $24.66 to $26.66 range. On a $1500 a month overdraft I was paying $31.50 a month and on the $500 overdraft I was paying $23.16 a month. So in overdraft alone in a year I was paying approximately $655.92 and just by having overdraft protection I would have been saving $64 a year. So why wouldn't everyone just have overdraft protection? Well, in my case the bank never told me about it and I did not take the time to properly educate myself about it. I did not know it was an option. Also, if that bank is raking in extra money due to my negligence, why would they say anything? They are a business and their goal – first and foremost – is to make money.

The last minimum fee we need to talk about is monthly banking fees and annual credit card fees. For the reason that, this is another area in which the bank is taking advantage of low income earners. Now keep in mind that bank fees are going to vary depending on the type of chequing account that you are currently using as well as the bank you are with. So what we are going to do is work with averages. Generally speaking, a low-end chequing account will allow you to do ten transactions per month at a cost of $4 per month, thus $48 per year. (This is a rough estimation. Some accounts allow you to do more and some less depending upon the bank.) However, anytime you go over ten transactions every proceeding transaction is going to cost you a dollar. Now a ten transactions maximum is extremely low. Let's say you get paid by cheque and not through direct deposit. Depositing two cheques a month amounts to two of your transactions, paying your rent or mortgage is a third, your power bill is the forth, sewer and water is the fifth, phone bill is the sixth, vehicle insurance is the seventh, gas the eighth and then you still have all of your other bills. Your credit card and/or line of credit takes you to ten transactions and this does not even include getting food or going out and having a life. So what's the next best thing? How about twenty-five transactions a month? This will – on average – cost you $10 per month so already that is roughly a 120 percent increase in cost and going to cost you $120 per year as opposed to $48. OK, now let's say twenty-five transactions a month is not enough (because it was not for me), so you go unlimited transactions. Surprise, this is going to cost you $15 per month, $180 per year and amount to roughly a 50 percent cost increase from the last upgrade and an over 300 percent increase from the basic chequing account. So here is the secret to reducing costs here: figure out how often you do transactions. If you do 30 transactions a month and have the lowest account you will need to upgrade. Although $4 per month sounds great, you are actually spending $20 a month extra on your account in

transaction fees, so you may as well go one or two levels up and save yourself the extra $5-12, because over a year that adds up and when your income is low every single dollar counts.

The Credit Card Myth

There is a widely accepted and common misconception that you need a credit card in order to build your credit score. The most common misconception is that you must have an interest-based credit card from which you borrow money from your bank in order to build your credit score and credit history. Credit cards do help build your credit score however, you do not need a credit card that carries a monthly balance nor one that charges you a monthly interest rate to build your credit rating. So, this begs the question: without an interest-based credit cards how can you be expected to make on-line purchases such as buying this book or booking a vacation while still creating a good credit history and a better credit score? In order to do any of those things wouldn't you need a traditional based credit card? The answer in fact is both yes and no. Many banks have created an option for consumers to avoid having a debt-based credit card. The type of credit card we will be referring to is known as a secured credit card and it has all the same functionality as a traditional credit card minus the owing money or paying interest aspects. So why haven't you heard of this before or if you have why don't you have one? The fact is banks don't care if you do or do not know about it. If you are willing to get a traditional credit card and pay huge interest rates, the banks are more than happy to take your money. Think about it, do you honestly believe that banks post profits of a billion dollar every quarter by keeping you informed? No, of course not. The bank makes money by keeping people in the dark and by getting as much money from customers as possible. While the consumer thinks they are getting a great deal like, "I get Air Miles by using my credit card," or "Look, I get one percent cash back," the banks are cashing in on your hard earned money. All of these supposed benefits are negated by interest rates and annual fees so stop kidding yourself. The features that are set up by the bank are not intended to help you out; they are intended to make the banks more money. Now, in all seriousness, if you have a traditional credit card destroy it! (Cut it up. Freeze it in a bucket of ice. Put it in the bottom of the kitty litter box.) Do something that will keep you from using it! Instead, use the previously discussed methods of lowering your

interest rates.

You can get two different types of credit cards that do not require any debt or debt loaded features. The first one being the credit chequing card which literally just allows your regular bank card to function as a credit card. Ergo, you can book hotels and trips and buy things on-line. The second option is what we touched on previously, the secured credit card. A secured credit card does not have the function of going into the red (aka owing money to the bank) meaning that you can only use it when you load money onto it. You cannot get yourself in debt related trouble with this type of card as you can only make purchases when you can afford them. This is going to help make you a vastly more informed consumer. Having one of these types of credit cards will also help build or rebuild your credit score and you do not need to

enter into debt. Merely by using a secured credit card the bank notes that you have a good credit history and do not transfer a monthly negative balance. Thus, you are a person whom they would like to lend money to. That is what a credit score does. The higher your credit score, the more likely the bank is willing to give you money. Plain and simple.

Credit score is also an important item we need to discuss. There are a lot of misconceptions behind how to and how not to build your credit score. A lot of people will tell you that you need a credit card or overdraft to build credit. Let me be the first to tell you that this way of thinking is wrong. If you pay rent or power or have a cell phone you are currently building your credit score. (Paying bills on time helps build your credit score). The number one thing that is going to negatively affect your credit score is either only paying the minimums which means carrying a balance forward from month to month or by missing payments. Another scary thing that affects your credit sore (which I found out the hard way), is carrying a negative balance on a cancelled credit card. As long as you have an active credit card and are making a payment higher than the minimum you are going to have a positive effect on your credit. The second you cancel that credit card that still has a negative balance the bank looks at it as non-essential debt and every month regardless of what you pay is going to have a negative effect on your credit score until that balance hits zero. That is why you want to destroy your credit card but not cancel it. The second you hit a zero balance then cancel it and you will negate any negative affect that would have occurred had you canceled it first.

Finally, (Just to beat you over the head) credit cards have fees attached to them and those fees are what's really getting the better of you. Most credit card have a minimum $30 a year fee. If you tack that onto all the other fees we have talked about you are starting to get into the realm of ridiculous. Like all other fees, credit card fees are negotiable and once you stop using a credit card you can get into an account that has no fees. Start making payments higher than your minimum and you start building a higher credit score. A higher credit score allows for more negotiating power and more negotiating power means lower interest rates and lower interest rates mean less money leaving your pocket each month.

After all the immediate bills are paid for on a low income salary there is already zero dollars left over to start paying things down. Decreasing minimum payments and lowering monthly fee expenses is going to make a big difference. Freeing up even $30 a month, by using any of these tactics, will go a long way toward helping you get out of debt. When starting out with little to no extra money to pay things off, the process will seem slow and daunting.

However, every extra payment made– even as little as $30 per month – is going to free up more money the preceding month and gradually make the process faster and easier.

Debt Repayment Methods and Emergency Funds

In this chapter we will be looking at the meat and potatoes of how to pay off your debt as well as how to build an emergency fund. An emergency fund is a daunting but crucial

undertaking. Often, most debt specialists will say you should have a fund that covers up to 6 months of expenses and if you cannot do that you should strive to have at least $500 in this fund. Well, assuming you just freed up that $30 a month as we talked about in the last chapter, both of those goals are going to seem nearly impossible. Stashing away all of your money and not paying down your debt is also not a good thing and at $30 a month it would take roughly

17 month to have $500 put away and a near lifetime to get 6 months' worth of expenses set aside. So what we're going to discuss in this chapter – with regard to building emergency funds – is to start with lower amounts outside of what is generally advised and build those amounts up as more funds become available.

What has been unbelievably successful for me has been setting short-term goals that are challenging but not unachievable. In regards to an emergency fund let's start by committing to building a $100 emergency fund within three months. Understandably, having little income makes this fairly difficult so you are going to have to get creative in order to get money into this account. Lots of people will advise you to sell unused stuff or have a garage sale to build up this fund but what if you don't have anything to sell? What you need to do instead is start putting any change you find into this account – anything from recycled bottles to coins you find on the street or (should you be so lucky) an unexpected bonus. If you receive any type of government assistance such as GST/HST cheques or child tax credits, child support, tax returns and any other type of money coming in outside of your regular work, use this to start building up your emergency fund. Try and commit at least 50 percent of any unexpected income into your emergency account. You should try to put more than 50 percent of this money in if possible, but you don't want to overdo it. Start building positive financial habits upon small successes. As you gain traction, it will be easier to have larger successes and work towards more challenging objectives. It is easy to become discouraged if you make your initial goals too big. Start with the intent of building a small emergency account fund and then later, commit to added additional fund that will be used for the purpose of debt repayment.

When it comes to debt repayment you need a strategy. You do not want to go in blind (aka no game plan). There are all types of different strategies and methods of debt repayment. You need to find out what works best for you and your situation. Also, if one method is not working, you can switch between multiple different methods. Once you start doing things one way you may find that it is not right for you or your situation has changed and thus you need a new plan of attack. The more flexible you can

be with your debt repayment strategies the

better your chances of becoming debt-free. We will

start by taking about the first method of attack

known as the Debt Snowball.

The Debt Snowball:

This method of repayment was created by American financial author, radio host, television personality and motivational speaker, **Dave Ramsey**. You start by writing down all of your debts and you rank each of your debts based upon the total amount owed from lowest to highest. Then you pay only the minimums on all of your debts excluding one. The lowest of your debts you will throw all of your extra money toward. Then as you pay off your lowest debt you transfer the minimum payment from the paid-off debt to your next debt plus the extra money you were using to pay off the last debt. Thus, small victories start building up more available funds, so that larger debts can have more allocated resources put towards them. Also by paying off the smallest debts there is the psychological effect of achieving a victory (I paid this bill off! It is possible to pay things off!). The advantage to this method is that it allows you to work on one bill at a time and this helps makes things feel a lot less intimidating. It is easier to deal with one bill that is say $500 as opposed to all your debt at once which could be a lot of money and look like an immovable mountain. You chip away little by little and the small successes constantly amplify until they become larger successes.

Debt Stacking Also Known as the Debt Avalanche:

This is also a popular method of paying off your debts. How debt stacking works is that again you make a list of all of your debts and with each debt you note the interest rates that you are paying on each debt. By way of example, let's say you have three credit cards each

carrying a balance. Debt A is for $2000 at 18 percent interest, Debt B is $8,000 at 12 percent interest and Debt C is for $1,000 at 9 percent interest. With a Debt Stacking method you would start by paying of Debt A. This is because it has the highest interest rate and is costing you the most money each month. Once debt A is paid off you'd tackle debt B then lastly you would pay of debt C. The thinking behind this method is that you are going to free up money quicker as well as it will prevent you from paying excessive amounts of in interest over time as you are getting rid of the highest interest rate debts first and thus ultimately saving money.

Debt Tsunami:

This is a method created by best-selling author and financial expert, Adam Baker. Baker is creator of the Man VS Debt program. Baker's mantra is: Sell Your Crap. Pay Off Your Debt. Do what you love. In a debt tsunami you need to rank your debts based upon the emotional impact that each corresponding debt has on your life. So, let's say you owe money on a credit card but you also owe money to a friend. So if the debt to friend is causing more emotional distress in your life then the credit card debt is then you will first pay off the friend and then move onto the next bill. The thinking behind this is that as you remove emotional impacts and stresses from your life you will become more confident and feel better about yourself as a person. (There is such a thing as financial self-esteem.) Thus, creating a situation in which there is

self-improvement happening within your life as well you are also paying down your debt load.

The Recession Proof Debt Snowball:

This method is similar to the Debt Snowball but with a few minor tweaks to it. Also, this is not a method I'd recommend using until after you have cleared up some debt and have more available funds to allocate towards your debts. With the recession-proof snowball you build up an emergency fund of $1,000 first then you save the entire balance of your first debt plus an additional $1,000. Thus, if your lowest debt is $400, you would first save up $2,400 and then pay off the bill in full before then move onto the next bill. The idea behind this is that you are building a sizable slush fund while still working through your debts and that you will have ample funds available if any unforeseen emergencies arise. Lastly, when all your debts have been repaid and if nothing came up, you have a sizable chunk of change in your savings account.

Debt Snow Flaking:

The idea behind Debt Snow Flaking is that anytime there is unexpected money that comes your way, you apply it your debts. Let's say you get a tax return – you put that money towards a debt. Maybe you sell stuff at a garage sale, get a rebate or find $10 on the street – everything and anything that is unexpected money – over and above your budget – you apply directly towards a bill. The idea is that a single snow flake does not build a snow ball but a snowball is built by snowflakes. Debt Snow Flaking works extremely well in decreasing your initial monthly payments when combined with any of the previously discussed debt repayment method. Let's say you are doing a Debt Avalanche as well as Snow

Flaking that debt at the same time. You are going to amplified your speed of debt repayment and get yourself free and clear of debt sooner.

Now that you have a handle on the types of debt repayment methods that exist, you need to figure out which method or combination of methods will work best for you and your situation. As well, once your situation changes you can reassess what method(s) you can use that will fit with your debt repayment plan and work best with your life and lifestyle.

Goal Setting and Budgeting

Now that you have strategies for how you are going to pay off your debts you need to start goal setting. This may sound unnecessary but goal setting is absolutely crucial. By writing things out, setting goals and planning you are able to track your progress. There are two types of budgeting and goal setting you need to keep in mind: long-term goals and short-term goals. When it comes to long-term goals, I found it works best if you set goals for the duration of the year so come next year you can see if you were able to achieve those goals and if not, why they eluded you. When it comes to short-term goals, it works best if you set them within a three month period and then every three months review your goals to see which ones you reached and which ones you didn't and the ascertain the reason(s) why. This is going to take some time and tweaking as you don't want to make goals so hard that you will never reach them but

neither do you want goals that are too easy to reach. What you need is a balance where goals are challenging yet achievable.

In your budget you will need to record exactly how much money you earn in one month then write down all your expenses bills, rent, car, phone and so on. Granted, you will need to get your income to debt ration to or below 100 percent, meaning there is now money left over in your budget after all your mandatory expenses have been covered. What you need to do is set a strict entertainment + food budget. I am not telling you to completely change your

lifestyle but what I am saying is you need to begin practising discipline. Once you have a budget set you need to keep within that budget. What I found worked best for me was physically

withdrawing the cash then putting it into jars that were labeled. You would have X money in your food jar and X money in your entertainment jar. You can cheat a little, if necessary. For example, if you use up your entire food budget you can transfer money out of your

entertainment jar into your food jar. The eventual, however, is that after each month there will be money left over in the jars. The left over money is then transferred over into your

 emergency fund jar in order to build that up or

"snowflake" onto other debts. Once that fund is built

up you can use excess money to put towards your

bills.

Budget example

Credit card debt $2,000 with a minimum

payment $40 a month, line of credit $11,000 with a

minimum payment of $120 per month, rent $1,000

per month, bank fees $40 a month and utilities $120

a month. Total cost per month: $1320. Now factor in

your wage at $10 an hour for 80 hours a month that

is $1,600 before taxes. Now minus what you pay in

taxes. Just to make this example easier to follow, we

will say you pay $100 a month in taxes. That leaves

you with $180. From this amount you will need to calculate your food and entertainment budget. This is going to change from person to person. But as a rule of thumb you want to choose an amount that will work within your means but still factor in the idea that you want to pay off your debt. Let us say $100 a month for food and $20 for entertainment. That leaves a remaining $60 to put towards your debt.

An easy 3 month goal would be to pay one of your bills down by $180 in 3 months. That will require putting the full $60 per month onto your bills. Challenge yourself a little here. Instead, try to pay off $200 in three month. By setting the bar slightly higher, it is going to mean that you are going to have to come up with an extra $20 for bill repayment. This could come from budgeting differently or by trying to earn some more money from your job. By setting

financial goals that are slightly more difficult it should entice you to set other goals on this budget sheet that are not necessarily related to your finances.

Goal lists should also include methods of bettering yourself. It is not always just about money. Sometimes doing things that will make you feel better about yourself are going to greatly heighten your ability to reach your financial goals. Thus, a goal list should include things like: read more or cook at home more often, get in better shape or spend more time with your family. You should also include on this list ways in which you are working towards your passions. Do these goals both long and short-term. Have your personal goal list for the year but then also set goals for every three months. It is no secret that self-esteem and personal

happiness play a major role in debt repayment. If you are unhappy or unsure about yourself it is going to be easier for you to let your goals slide and your budget fall apart. Becoming happy and taking responsibility for your actions has just as much to do with becoming debt-free as does the financial aspect of it. The last point I want to touch on (and it may sound obvious) is not to throw out your goal lists once they have been completed. I carry my goal list with me in my wallet. Once my goal list has been achieved, I create a new one and carry that one with me. I save all he old goal lists so that I may look back and review my progress. This gives me a better

snapshot of my progress and helps with future goal

setting. I am able to look back on what worked and

what didn't and incorporate new insights into future

goal setting. It is also great to look back on where

you were six months ago and see how the

achievement of those goals helped you get to where

you are now.

Change you are Thinking, Do your Research and Surround yourself with the Right People

Your mindset and how you think about money is going to be a crucial factor in your ability to maintain a budget and to have the willpower to pay off your debts. Saving money is not just about being frugal or abstaining from things you enjoy – though both are certainly parts of the equation. It has more to do with becoming a happy person and a smarter consumer. The constant bombardment of ads and new products being thrown at us day in and day out has helped create a society of rampant consumerism. As well, the ability to easily get more credit has led droves of people into over-consuming and buying more then they need or require. This was me at one point. Does it also sound like you today?

There are a lot of easy

tactics that you can implement in order to change

your thinking when it comes to what you need verses

what you want. The first thing is – if you are trying to

pay off your credit cards and debts – do not use your

credit cards or unexpected income to make

purchases. Second, when you do buy something,

saves up for it and buys it in cash when you have the

money to do so. Of course, you cannot always buy

everything in cash such as a mortgage on a house, a

student loan payment or a car payment. For things

you need to borrow money for car make sure you

are getting into something that is within your means.

A four bedroom house with three

bathrooms is not a sensible purchase if there will

only two of you living there. I know of a childless couple who live with their small dog in a 4000 square foot, five-bedroom home (with five bathrooms). And sadly, they are by no means in the minority. You need to understand what you need and what you can afford and live within your means, meaning that you live off of what you earn. Put quite simply, don't acquire more debt just because you want something.

So what if you are currently living beyond your means? Let's say that my four bedroom example relates back to you or you have an expensive car that you are locked into for 84 months making payments. Here's the painful truth, you are broke and cannot afford it and if you don't make a change you are going to remain broke. With the large house consider getting roommates to help pay down the mortgage or sell your house and move somewhere more affordable. If you are renting also look for roommates or downgrade. Now what about that car? Well, either try to work it into one of your repayment methods so that eventually you are paying more than the minimums on it in order to clear the debt load up faster, return it or trade it in for something that you can afford. Keep in mind, there will be a point where you owe more on that expensive car than what it is worth. It is called negative equity. Few vehicle appreciate in value. Most depreciate by as much as ten percent the moment you leave the car lot. And far too many people – wanting a new vehicle every couple years –

will roll over the outstanding balance into the purchase of a new vehicle. You can see where this leads – to disaster.

When your debt-free and have built up some savings that is when you can start considering some higher-end luxuries. But for now you need to get your thinking in alignment with reality. By accepting the reality of your situation you can adjust your lifestyle to fit that situation. It doesn't mean you are going to like it, but you need to take responsibility for it. Once you adjust to living within your means, a very positive and interesting thing begins to occur, you are able to start improving your situation and can alter and shift your reality slowly towards what you want from life. Being debt-free is a powerful state-of-being that allows you to stop working that job you hate or doing things that make you miserable. It gives you the time and energy to start moving in the direction you want to go. I am not trying to sound like a

self-help book here but the reality is that self-esteem and money are synonymous with one another in many aspects and good budgeting requires good discipline and self-esteem.

Nevertheless, there will be barriers that will slow you down and you need to know what those barriers are and how to deal with them. A common issue when trying to budget is

learning how to say no to your family and friends. This is important because how often are you invited out by family and friends to do things that cost money? For example: going out for food, coffee, drinks, movies and so on and so forth. Nobody wants to say, "Sorry, I cannot come out. I am broke." Instead, it might be simply and more accurate to say, "I cannot come out because I am trying to save money and pay down my bills." If your friends cannot understand that then you may need to be reconsidering your friendships. Remember, you can still go out and do things and have fun but it needs to fit within the entertainment budget you set for yourself. So, either make plans in advance that will fit that budget or use the fund for sporadic fun times but when it is all used up you need to stop going out – period.

The reason why we are touching on this topic has to do with the fact that more often than not if you are dealing with financial difficulties then likely so are the people that hang around you. They may not say it, or you might not perceive it, but it is highly likely. Thus, if they are not budgeting and planning on improving their situation then they are still likely in a state of debt addiction. It is fine to hang out with these people but don't support their spending behaviours and don't allow them to negatively affect yours. If you have friends or family who are excellent with their money and budgeting, then spend more time with them as their

positive role modeling will have positive effects on you. And they will be able to help keep you motivated in your mission to stay on a budget and become debt-free. There's a famous French proverb that goes something like this, "Show me whom you frequent and I will tell you who you are." So start

frequenting (spending time with) people who are

going to help you and improve your situation. Just

for the purpose of over explanation, imagine you are

a long distance runner and there are two different

people you can hang out with. Person "A" being

someone who has no interest in running at all and

person "B" who is also a long distance runner.

Obviously,

person "A" is not going to help you become a better

runner, whereas person "B" will be

someone to compete against and train with and in

turn improve your running ability. Budgeting and

managing your finances works in the exact same

manner. By spending time with people who are going

through the same experience as you or who have

already had success, you are going to create an environment where you are positively influenced by those around you and will also be able to learn from their experiences. This also leads in nicely into our next topic.

Educate yourself and do your research. With any new venture you are starting it is important to become as knowledgeable as possible on the topic. When I first started budget planning I had little interest in reading personal finance books. Instead, I began reading blogs and newspaper articles on the topic and as my knowledge base grew, I then moved into reading personal finance books, planning books, self-esteem, marketing and essentially anything I could get my hands on that had to do with improving my financial situation. The importance of

educating yourself on the topic is to create a good

foundation of knowledge. This way you can more

easily work through the hard times but also use

different ideas and methods to tweak your own

budget in order to make it more functional with your

life and situation. The more you know the better

your execution is going to be and the more likely you

will be able to become debt-free and have the

proper information to inform others how to do the

same.

Part of educating yourself is to help change

your way of thinking when it comes to

money. In today's modern society it is no surprise to

anyone that we live in a consumer based society that

tries to manipulate the notion of need versus wants.

What do we need in life? Just thinking at a bare minimum here. We need food, cloths, shelter and happiness. Now, there are certain wants that can end up also being required in order to achieve our needs. For example, you may in fact need a vehicle in order to get to work to earn money to fulfill your needs. What you can control here is the type of vehicle. Do you need the best and greatest vehicle to get to and from work or do you just need something that does the job? When it comes to making purchases on items you must ask yourself, "Is this a need or is this a want?" If It is a want is it worth keeping you in the financial situation you are in even longer then you need to be. Does said want make your life exponentially better based upon the cost that is going into it? If it doesn't then you should likely avoid getting it. This doesn't mean you cannot treat yourself to something; you just need to begin to change your thinking when it comes to material objects. They are nice to have but they are non-essential. Lastly (and this may sound insane) but use money for things that have value added and most things that have value added to them are other people such as, helping pay for your kids' education or saving to go on trips with family and friends – build up your memories, not your stuff. Helping out your family or your friends is going to bring more happiness into your life than any new gadget ever will. Don't believe me? Try it out for a bit and I am a 100 percent certain you will start believing me.

Become Indispensable

Have you ever heard any of these expressions before? Work smarter not harder, work more/earn more and if all else fails work elsewhere? An important way to improve your budget is to earn more money. Mind you, this easier said than done. If you are currently earning

minimum wage there are likely several factors as to why that is the case. You may just be

entering the work force, just started a new job, economy is in the dumps and you could not find any other job, you are not confident in your skills to look for a better paying job and lastly, maybe your just not the best employee. In this chapter, we'll work through each of the aforementioned situations and come up with ways that will make you indispensable to your employer and allow you to start earning more money. Switching jobs is not always an option but staying with your current employer does not mean that you cannot start earning more money.

The concept of working smarter not harder is something you should be doing if you are not already. Obviously, working smarter will be different for every job, but there are basic concepts that can be applied to any form of employment. Figure out what exactly needs to be done in your job from day-to-day as well as throughout the weeks and months then start by scheduling out your day and the things that need to get accomplished. In this schedule figure out what the most effective manner of execution is going to be. For example, if I do "A" first then "B" will happen a lot faster as opposed to if I do "B" first "A" will take longer. Think back to the previous chapter and the importance of doing your research. Likely, there are people you work with who excel at what they are doing and make it look easy. Start asking them for help and advice as this will make you more effective at the job and save you energy.

Next is the concept of work more. This is fairly straightforward. If you can pick up more shifts at your job you should do so. If you recall, our initial "freed up" amount of income was only $30 so picking up even three more hours in the month could potentially double the amount of free income you will have to work with each month. Of course, you need to consider your current financial and personal situation. It is easier for a single person to pick up more hours of work as opposed to someone with a family. Thus, if you have the ability to pick up plenty of extra shifts, do it. If your ability to work more is limited by having a family, try to

figure out a way in which you can pick up a more work without sacrificing time with your family perhaps working while the kids are in school or when you have availability of a babysitter.

You need to be earning what you are worth. If you feel that this is not happening then you need to consider working elsewhere. Even if you are not looking or do not want a different job, start right now as you should always be scouting out new work opportunities. Sometimes switching to a new job for the same amount of money can be a positive change. For example, if you can find a job that has benefits such as medical or prescription coverage this can go a long way and free up potential money. Also a healthy state-of-mind is important if you are feeling dragged down and dread getting up in the morning for work then it time for a change. Work related stress can have a negative impact on your health and mental state and sometimes just switching jobs can go a long way in helping you out. Being in a positive mental state means you are less likely to get sick and be more in control of your life thus making it less likely to impulse spend or spend to make yourself feel better. When switching work, make sure to leave your current job on a high note. If or when you give your notice, do not coast through your last few days.

In fact, do the opposite: work the hardest you ever have because later on in life that positive reference may pay dividends in your ability to find future employers.

Moving back now to a previous point, if you are currently in a job that you cannot or do not want to leave but you are still making low income you need to reflect on yourself and determine why your wage has not increased to where you would like it to be. This plays into the idea of becoming indispensable. You need to become the best employee. First, figure out how to work smarter and from there start becoming passionate about your work so that everyone who works with you or customers whom deal with you know that you are a person who gets things done. The major advantage to this is it gives you the ability to ask for more money. I guarantee you that if you are a star on the team, the company will always find extra money to send your way. A raise that is as small as only 50 cents per hour can go a long way toward helping to reduce your debt. For example, in an 80 hour work week 50 cents per hour will add an extra $40 to your biweekly paycheque and an extra $80 to your monthly income. A budget that originally only had $30 available now has $110 available which means your bills are now getting close to being paid down at a rate four times faster than before. When it comes to money and budgeting, every single cent counts and you want to strive to get any amount of extra money into your budget. A small amount over

the course of a year can go a long way!

Debt Fatigue

When it comes to paying off debt on a low income, you are going to be in it for the long haul. Plenty of books will tell you that you can be debt-free is just a few months but the reality for most people is even with lots of discipline reaching financial freedom is years away. Debt fatigue is highly likely when you are paying debt over a long period of time and refers to when a person becomes overwhelmed by their debt load and the amount of time they have spent

paying down their debt. Debt fatigue is often accompanied by a feeling of hopelessness in which the person stops paying down their debts and begins to start to re-accumulate debt. This may eventually reinforce the idea that bankruptcy is the only feasible option and accumulated debts no longer matter at that point. When it comes to debt fatigue there are telltale signs that you are suffering from it and fortunately, methods to alleviate it and get yourself back on track. In this chapter, we will be looking at both the symptoms and solutions you can use to combat debt fatigue.

An early sign of debt fatigue is when you continuously find reasons to take small amounts of money away from debt repayment and add it to you entertainment or food budget. Or you start taking money out of your emergency fund to top up your budget because you

improperly spent. This may start off by being innocent ($5 here and $10 there) but it can quickly get out of control. If you are noticing that you

are rationalizing reasons to not put

money on your debt then you are likely suffering

from early stages of debt fatigue. But do not fret as

there are several tactics to combat this condition.

First, reflect back onto your goals as to see

why you started paying off your debt in the first

place. Is the item you are planning on buying worth

the additional debt or the slowing down of your

repayment program? Also, if you are having trouble

with impulse buying tries to avoid having money on

your person for a while to stave off making frivolous

purchases.

Another thing that can help is going to friends or

family who can offer you support (The type of friends

and family that will not try to convince you to spend

money). Lastly, and this is only an option if you are really struggling, you may need to consider a short-term debt vacation.

What is a debt vacation? A debt vacation is when you decide that you are really struggling with the amount of money going out and your inability to do what you want. So, instead of slowly slipping into debt fatigue you reset you budget for one month. You figure out all of your minimums and what you owe for that month and then all remaining money goes into your personal budget for you to spend on yourself. Now, most financial advisors will tell you that this is not a good idea. When the debt vacation ends you must go right back to paying down your bills. The rationale behind this is that entering a period of full-on debt fatigue will be far more damaging then take a month off to revaluate your situation. Keep in mind that the goal is to get out of debt so do not start taking a debt vacation every few months. This should only ever be used if you are really struggling and should be limited to once or twice a year at the most.

Debt can be draining and monotonous, especially when you are earning a low income. This is because you are going to be in it for quite some time. Make sure to take care of yourself and make sure to regularly revaluate your goals and your plans to remain motivated. Debt is hard thing to get out of and it will not be an easy journey. Make sure to keep yourself

surrounded by people who support you and have similar goals.

What to do if you are in the midst of full on debt fatigue? You have stopped paying down bills as you are now off your budget and going backwards and back into debt. The first thing to do is to stop spending money that you do not have. You can take comfort in the fact that you had been doing everything right up until the point you started suffering from debt

fatigue. Consequently, when you start redoing the previous steps from the beginning you need to determine what the reasoning was that you entered into debt fatigue. Was your budget too tight? Did you have the wrong people around you? Did you miss something in your budget? Did a situation take place in your life that changed your plans – personal or professional? Pinpoint the reason to why things went wrong. When you are setting up your goals, do some

pre-planning. Expect some debt fatigue so come up with methods and tactics to avoid or deal with the problem in the future. Also set up a budget and game plan that works for your new situation. If things were too hard the first time around, make an easier-to-utilize budget and slowly increase debt repayment at a rate that you can manage. Things' taking longer is not

always a bad thing. If by slowing things down it helps you stay on track then you are more likely to reach your goals as opposed to if you try to rush things and they just keep going sideways.

Remember back to the section of the emergency fund? Life will absolutely throw a wrench into your plan from time to time. If there are more factors in your life then just your debt, make sure that you are still making time to solve these problems and making allowances for them in your plan. If you need to divert more money for emergencies then do so. But

remember, whatever you do make sure that the end goal is to improve your situation and to eventually get out of debt.

What to do when you are starting to get ahead finally

So you may not be debt-free yet but things are starting to clear up. Debt is reducing and maybe income is increasing. So should you continue sending all of you extra money on to debt or are there other options now? The great thing about this situation is there are all kinds of

options available to you. You can keep throwing all the extra onto your debt or you can start working on a few other choices that are going to help keep you debt-free once your journey in debt is coming to an end.

Something important that you can start diverting some money to is your emergency savings account. Once you have some extra money (and if you can pull this off) you need to make sure this account has a standing balance of at least $500 and then consider growing this amount. Often a solid emergency saving account has about six months' worth of expense

within it. This account can prove to be extremely important if you fall on hard times so consider moving some money over here.

Another great idea which incorporates making and saving money is diverting some of your additional funds to your retirement plan. The great thing about this is when you put

money into your retirement plan you can also claim it on your taxes. This is a win-win situation. You create savings while potentially increasing your tax return at the end of the year. The additional tax money can then be reinvested or used to it pay off more bills or increases your emergency fund. By doing one you create a situation where you can speed up another avenue.

Lastly, consider investing into yourself. You can use extra money to take courses or go to school then use these skills to find yourself better paying jobs. Or if you have a hobby you are passionate about, you can invest the money into that and improve your quality of life while putting money into yourself. Education and betterment is always going to make things in your life better and can help with you reaching your debt goals and your personal goals faster. And once again (just to beat it over the head) you can use this money to pay off your debt even faster which will can improve the quality of your life dramatically. Whatever it is you decide to do with your money, make sure you choose something that is going to improve your situation.

How to Stay Debt-free

Staying debt-free is just as important as becoming debt-free. But as with anything, there are going to be some difficulties and information you will need to know in order to maintain a debt-free lifestyle. The number one key thing to remain debt-free is fairly simple: spend less then you make and you will never end up in debt again. Additionally, make sure to pay yourself first. Generally, when it comes to paying yourself first you should be looking at putting away roughly ten percent of your paycheque into savings ever pay period. However, if other

expenses do not allow you to put that much away, make sure to budget in another amount. Saving as little as $20 a paycheque can add up quickly. If you are paid bi-weekly, for example, you will have saved $520 in one year. If you are paid twice a month, that adds up to $480 in a year. Plus, the more you are putting into savings, the more your money will start working for you and create the ability to generate additional income to make your life far more comfortable.

Think like a rich person. A great quote from Warren Buffet goes something like this: "Someone is sitting in the shade today because someone planted a tree a long time ago." When it comes to money and accumulating money, you need to be thinking long-term. If you are only thinking about your money in the now (day-by-day) then you will have an incredibly difficult time getting ahead in the future.

Just to expand upon Warren Buffet's quote here, if you want to live a carefree, debt-free life then plant the seeds now, nurture them and help them grow. By paying off your debt, you will have found and created an area in which you can now accumulate wealth and live the life you desire. But there is more to it than just being debt-free. You need to take all the lessons you have learned about budgeting and rethinking money and translate that into saving and wealth building. Start setting money aside for the future and making plans for your future and you will grow a beautiful tree that stays with you and provides shade for the rest of your life. You will instil positive financial thinking into your children, you will motive your family and friends and you will be able to invest into yourself and reach your goals.

Money is merely a means to an end within our society but we need to have it in order to do certain things and to live our lives. But we need not be ruled by it. Instead, rule your money and create a future that does not involve debt. Become free from your shackles of debt and start truly living your life to the fullest.